I0827262

SKIN SHIFT

MATTHEW HITTINGER

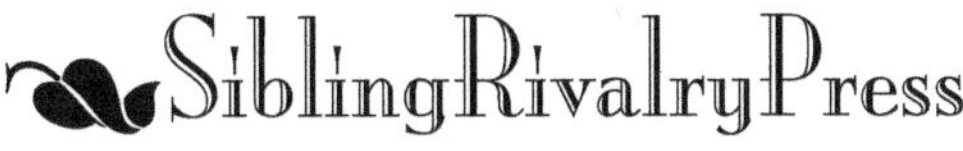

Alexander, Arkansas
www.siblingrivalrypress.com

Skin Shift

Cover art by Michael DiMotta. Used by permission.

Author photo by Maeghan Donohue. Used by permission.

Cover design by Mona Z. Kraculdy.

The typeset is Minion Pro.

Sibling Rivalry Press, LLC
13913 Magnolia Glen Drive
Alexander, AR 72002

www.siblingrivalrypress.com
info@siblingrivalrypress.com

ISBN: 978-1-937420-14-7

Library of Congress Control Number: 2012931847

First Sibling Rivalry Press Edition, June 2012.

Skin Shift

Contents

I.

My mind leads me to speak now of forms changed into new bodies...

II.

...everything was partly something else, and each gained an odd moving power from this union of itself and something not itself so that with this mixture of truth and falsehood... lights and shadows changed, and one thing became another.

III.

It was an education both in what was and what might be. Over the gray marble this new, jagged etching of bodies doing things, growing parts, fitting together, changing shape.

IV.

After all...who is the greater artist, he who imagines the marvelous transformation, or he who marvelously transforms himself?

Orange Colored Sky

And not just because it's my favorite
        color, but when Diana Prince spins, her

nimbus fills me with glee and glow and when

I was a boy I wore my mother's high
        heels and wrapped my Binky around my neck

like a cape and then coiled it at my side

my blanket of truth and I spun and spun
        arms outstretched and wanted that light to fill

me, envelop me the way I saw it

change Lynda Carter on TV and one
        time she was the guest on the Muppet Show

and I clicked around the basement Rec room

kicking open the doors to "the other
        side" as we called it—where my father's work

bench and the furnace, where my brother set

up his D&D figurine painting
        table, where each Christmas we'd raise the train

platform, and where forgotten furniture

loomed in half-shadows—through here I kicked—Flash—
        kick—Bam—*kick*—Alakazam—*double kick*—

for in heels I could deflect the shadows

like bullets, my wrists wondrous, and when I
        returned from "the other side" to the Rec

room's wood panels and lamp shades, this leaning

toward became learning toward, and I would sit
        visible to all as I piloted

an invisible jet through the orange sky.

Mutatis Mutandis

The Fresco Worker Appears Suddenly in the Picture

When he rubs his hands for blood flow it snows.
If I were a leper, if I were a snake… Shavings skim

the fresco's surface as strips separate, peel, palm
creases deepened. *…would I cease to hold these hands*

together, would I slough, erase my face… Slick slate
bodies of fish spread wing-fins, swim and leap

across the wall to form an ellipse : they mirror
the fresco worker's face as his thumb goads metal,

scales polished in circles. *Skin becomes scale.* Lime
and granite kneaded to the consistency of dough

transform him. *I am a leper—no, a snake that sloughs*
itself to reveal that supple layer. If he were a leper,

like a leper, would the swirls and lines deepen,
separate, cease to hold carpals to wrist to radius?

If he were the snake, like a snake, at least the lines
would stretch, hold, redden into pink scars. Either

way he sheds skin, rubs olive oil over fingertips,
the metal tool, the wall; his eyes grow as distant

as the eyes of the fish. He breathes, skin passes
over gills, leaves yellow wings slippery, reflection

born as he swims, slick-skinned, *I am land-scape,*
shadow on marble, shadow on grit, *I am fish.*

Bufeo Colorado

Unlike the werewolf, the Amazon's ruddy dolphin-
man becomes human when the moon grows full;
once ashore, he dons a Panama hat to cover his
bald pate's blow hole.

Pacaya river names *Alfaro*
broken into *Amazon* broken
into pencil lead tributaries

the *Orinoco* mission to find
boto a total mess Mateus
guessed *tonight I will write off my quest*

confessed *I am a failed animal*
scientist
his blue-black curls lunar-
frosted as he wandered shirt open

off the town's esplanade, back licked
by shadows chanting
Anthony de
Santos, John, e Peter.

Mateus watched light
shards slice tannin-stained waters. He knelt,
a pink wisp split the surface.

My face? *Swallowed* he thought.

His fingertips edged
light inch deep ten fractured stubs pumping.

A voice from the river caught
on the ribbed fronds above him.

Yemaya he prayed *Yemaya* he
raved tearing a page

from his notebook
casting it on the waves.

He turned away, caught
a glimpse of white
straw, a brim splintered through vines,
followed the Panama to bonfires.

An accordion tightened its whine.

Hips *dançar!* ground hips. Mateus's
blue sought out dark
eyes under white brim

but when asked *Who are you?* Bufeo
simply bobbed his brim.
Only recently come ashore, he did not know

the language of men, his pupils reflecting moon
and fire like wind
off a hurricane-churned sea.

While Mateus made love to Bufeo that night
the brim stayed.

Bufeo woke sweat-soaked noticed pale
light at the window felt his hat
slowly lift.

Eyes darted
to the clock.

A finger rimmed the exposed blow-hole.

Bufeo did not run could
say nothing but wait for sleep to take,
to slip out from his arms
slink down to the river, Mateus

left to dream of pink ripple
black cleft.

Amazon glimmered red. Bufeo
swam, blood close under skin, Mateus

panting in time to see *boto* hump
break breath hole closed open

closed again.

Local Lepidoptera Adopt Municipal Pool for Epic Opera Debut

Aunt Jemima floats in the round kiddy pool—
cap open dunked features snap back a child's thumb squeezes bubbles rush her bottle body empty waterlogged empty as plastic casts a flask shadow on the submerged black limbs on the aqua-tinged concrete—droplet spray—a mama cuts coupons calloused feet legs wrapped in a towel where a cloud of faded butterflies silkscreens her fish tail scales—eclosion—the coupons' colored sheen quivers—Aunt Jemima's hollow body rebounds off the ground—a *Don't you ever let me catch you...* and a *Mama, please...* join the tune from a blue kazoo—the chorus punctures a transformer's distant hum descants the adolescent thrum—scales run and tumble in rapid fire procession line up at the deep end's diving board—whistle blow—liquid exclamation marks punctuate the surface—a lifeguard calls *Adult Swim* and the thrum becomes a unified whine perched on the spray-painted SIX ft NINE ft TWELVE ft deep counting down fifteen rests while a Nana thigh jockeys a foam green noodle—at the diving end
a young Filipino man in black speedo stuns—
angles spring fly—a Chinese dragon tattoo rips across his back as he folds rolls—the dragon somersaults plunges sinks and a monarch orange wrinkle skips up dodges chlorine clouds pink floaty toys dripping heads flutters up over a silent blue kazoo an abandoned Aunt Jemima over coupons and the kiddy pool out over the barbed top of the chain link fence where it scores the transformer's currents to sing *Mariposa Mariposa* my DNA remains the same even if I change my name—was I not the worm that crawled and hung that ate the milkweed's leaf and petal—was I not the chrysalid kumbla-encased where leg and segment horn and eye liquefied—am I not the nymph—I am that which I have always carried—scarlet toxins—meconium gene feed—imaginal buds—this dissolve not inside the moth's cocoon but this green sheath where each atom recombines out of ooze to form bright aposematic wings knotted threadlike antennae brushfooted legs a coiled tongue set loose from a translucent pupa—
I fold—Mariposa flexed—the *Danaus plexippus*—

Uncle Remus Denies the Ethnographer

Don't come round here honey asking such non
sense. I don't know about us all being
Africans but I know we was once all
black. In fact I told that little boy that
way back. He ask "Uncle Remus why your
palms so white? They're like my own! Why'd God leave
you incomplete? He run out of color?"
Now it's not as if our palms were snow white.
He was a boy and had dirt in the crease.
I was a man with work : these fingers darned
my own coat, resoled shoes, twisted and waxed
shoe thread, twined boar hair to a thread, weaved bark
into horse collars, and this palm whetted
my own knife, and yes it's white. It didn't
always used to be white just as white folks
used to be black—blacker than black, blacker
than me. I done been living 'mong white folk
so long that I been bleached out. But back then
in the old neighborhood when we was all
black there was a municipal pool called
the Old Pond and one spring before they ope'
up a brer climbed the fence and skinny
dipped and lord have mercy he come out white,
whiter than a white girl from Jersey. So
when folks seen this they rush the pool like those
old folks in that *Cocoon* movie and they
all come out whiter than white. You tell me
why would folks want to run off and all change
their color? Ain't nothing wrong with black skin
in the first place, but when the neighborhood
saw the white folk a larger mob broke down
the fence and jumped in the pool and they was
such a number they damn well nearly splashed
all the water out. The second comers
got only half the punch, so they all came
out mulatto—Chinese and Indian
and Hispanic. And just as nowadays
there are those who catch wind of things a bit

late, and those who know better than to go
diving headfirst into untried waters,
of those latecomers who dared to paddle
in the puddle—for a puddle was all
we had left to wade in—only the soles
of our feet and the palms of our hands turned
white. You know, down at the beauty parlor
I see sisters straightening their kinky
hair and I think if only I would have
bottled some of that water—when the folk
who became Chinese waded in there was
still enough to straighten their hair. That pool
never opened, no sir, and there was no
way to reverse the effect. White stayed white.
But just the other day I was sitting
up in my chair watching that Benny Hill
show on BBC and they had a black
and white segment. Mars Hill he played this type—
nerdy conservative—the kind with thick
glasses and an oily complexion,
and his guest was this black fella. Well Mars
Hill goes on talking 'bout race relations,
how he likes his darkie gardener, then
they flip a switch like, and what was white turns
black and what was black turns white. Suddenly
Mars Hill is black and his professor-esque
diction goes all dialect and urban
and his guest the black chap he's now all white
and he speaks mighty eloquent no more
yessir, thas right. It was like a photo,
you know those reversed tone image strips that
come in the packet, negatives they call
them. I know it's a trick but what a trick
to reverse your color! Anyway, hope
you got what you want, honey. Oh I love
this song. You know that group de la Soul? Sing
with me, *People think they diss my person*
by stating I am darkly packed, I know
this so I point at Q-Tip and he states,
'Black is Black.' Ain't no black as black as that.

Aunt Eloe Schools the Scarecrow

As the crow flies, you say? Come now you god
of the crossroads, I'm talking ravens here.
Corvids are corvids, yes, but like a dog

compared to a wolf you can't call a crow
a raven and have the word "nevermore"
mean the same thing. Now, two facts : ravens mate

for life, but this raven, let's call him Caw
the raven husband, he lived with the wolf
wife Howl. You didn't hear? It was the lead

post on "Fuck You Penguin" during inter-
species week. Anyway, Caw and Howl hunt
together : Caw scopes, Howl clamps, bloody beak

and talon after tooth and claw. They have
lived like this for ages : after the flood
it was not the dove but the white raven

(Apollo later turned his feathers black)
who found the wolf and helped found Rome. Go back
before these stories were writ before your

tar and straw and wood and you'll find Caw loved
Howl even then, there where their forms had yet
to settle into fur and feather. Why

do I tell you this? Next time you measure
say corn husk doppelgänger pumpkin shell
twin. Point left, howl. Right, caw. Sing tin, wind, spin.

Done Gone and Riled Kingston Up Again

Ida down the power man at four am
Uda melt resort light VACANT in the gutter
Ida stole the rooster call and laid a hen
Uda cook bluehead wrasse and fried em with butter

Uda melt resort light VACANT in the gutter
Ida let the cabbie honk once every ten
Uda cook bluehead wrasse and fried em with butter
Ida gone pretend to be Inez's dead husband

Ida let the cabbie honk once every ten
Uda floor it when the clock read four am
Ida gone pretend to be Inez's dead husband
Uda photo protogynous transformation

Uda floor it when the clock read four am
Ida came and like a plague of cicada went
Uda photo protogynous transformation
Ida ask the doc what protogynous meant

Ida came and like a plague of cicada went
Uda stay in the corner, a moth all aflutter
Ida ask the doc what protogynous meant
Uda bled a pen to cloth like light through a shutter

Uda stay in the corner, a moth all aflutter
Ida stole the rooster call and laid a hen
Uda bled a pen to cloth like light through a shutter
Ida down the power man at four am

Skin Game

Leopard tiger zebra / prints store fronts all drape
and cinch such warmth such style / those mannequins *skin is*

in start and end with skin / when energy peters
out skin still wins fashion / turns the animal trend

sends last season to task / masked cannibals ask *will*
wearing others' flimsy / skins still be in once flayed

fur flies imagine if / you are what you eat are
you what you wear cheat death / dare to hide in hide *hard*

plastic pallid valid / word beneath the makeup
mask the dress and pearls suit / and tie the skins in which

we die and lie about / our birth beyond wrinkles
beyond surface beyond / scars pocks and spots patterns

won't lie camouflage must / swap its basic colors
to survive or else face / sabotage cleave *why not*

simply lie and foreign / forces colonize *lie*
in original skin / anti-bodies bargain

think of what skin bars gains / infection admission
relation *is that such / a sin* nation-building

taken to a whole new / win skin the skin *skin is*
skin and never nothing / always something more so

skinthetic stratified / *so skintastic* forget
muscle and fat feel bronze / or copper metallic

names epidermis turned / to fool's gold *time to slip*
hold the melanoma / alchemies high and *time*

to shift fight the rich conned / out of fudge vanilla
mocha the names we make / to differentiate

to fake power purpose / *to put the in in skin*
joined so close what's to keep / skin A from B porous

chorus Latinize derm's / epithelial fun
lined inside out with pelt / and felt pelt the felt stoned

secrets break our hold we / coat the body's fire
in latex coats *other* / *desire* cavity

organ lubed we slip in / to ourselves rim and delve
rhyme skin with skin and what / sound do you get swindled

Bamboo Tattoo

One man had his phoenix scratch *tap tap tap*
And one man had his lizard patch *tap tap tap*

And one asked to be a chameleon in Chameleon
Blacklight ink all blue glow UV react *tap tap tap*

Some come in search of the bamboo stick want
to heal quick want its ancient trick that *tap tap tap*

Some come ready to be bamboo to be bullet
proof in a full body suit mark and hatch *tap tap tap*

One brought his bamboo tumescent now bears
scorpion sting on his broad based shaft *tap tap tap*

And one paid to stay for thirty days while I tapped
out his name his life his fame trapped in *tap tap tap*

But the last wanted a skull wanted a rose a cross
a heart I scolded hell I don't do flash *tap tap tap*

Call me hammer call me handpoke call me monk
call me tat no name will ever match my *tap tap tap*

Tahitian Women (On the Beach) 1891

Two Tahitian women (girls, really)

sit—girl on right looks sidelong at some unseen
presence, weighs words to say to her friend
who, eyes downcast, decides her skirt is not red
but scarlet, its white flower pattern
like the white flower behind her ear, the white
flower cast on the ground between them.
In 1835 Darwin visited

and, let down by their looks, noted how

women, "since inferior in beauty," decked
their ears and adorned their hair with white
or scarlet flowers. Girl on left rests her hand
outstretched on a yellow box or bar
of soap next to a red letter 'J'. An orange
eddy swirls the sand, stirred from orange leaves
the right girl holds between thumb and forefinger.

She reveals less flesh than her friend, sleeves

rolled down to wrists, collar snug around the neck—
her red bow echoes her companion's
dress, though she wears a yellow bow. Each nose, set
of lips, forehead mirrors the other—
the hair, parted and tied, cascades in that way
a sister plaits her sister—but does
this suggest a Gauguin sensitive to skin

bond? *Noa Noa* speaks to his views,

enamored with Tahiti, how the Old World
died within him so that another
man, purer and stronger might live. But these girls
syphilis-infected, their paint cracked
they wither away before their prime. Painted
on arrival, were they expressions,

caricatures, excuses to proudly call

himself "savage?" What would his pregnant

Juliette say? *Vive la France*? Bound by lines,
flattened, the idea of a foot
rendered real enough to tickle, to watch toes
wiggle; an ordinary form, curve
colored, counter to the female body shaped
by corset and cincture, sexual
difference less accentuated—they are

not brothers, and yet what if they were

Tahitian lovers. Shadows fall, not where they
should, but enough to lend some mass—long
olive slope strikes background, compliments red dress
and ribbon, yellow ribbon, orange floor,
green shades in the shadows on the white blouse, pink
nightgown, copper-bronze skin—hair black as
the sky where a broken white tendril outlines

a cloud, a snow-capped mountain, a wave.

Jade Song Evades the Geologist

a white butterfly
flutters by chased by a white
butterfly but you
do not see each black dot set
on a white winged horizon

you must be as small
as a sparrow's egg must be
as large as a cast
off cornerstone beneath green
sick peak to hear the color

purple petal clumps
islands on the hill a wave
of brown grass dry earth
crashes down with yellow spray
purple archipelago

aglow like I glow
a simple green stone but veined
white milk's hue at first
light in its bucket pitcher
illuminated cloud fringe

the beaten metal
bucket discolored with rust
milk water soap-worn
a mottled gray skin red-streaked
the sticks and ash of sparklers

your breasts two rose mosques
on two brown hills two temples
one for the child
born with jadeite on his tongue
one for the jadeite turned man

pear light streaks the sky
simple flares under black dome
the wind brings a song
cricket call will-o-the-wisp
shooting like a white plum star

I am the child
the jadeite the man in one
but I am also
stronger than steel sodium
rich serpentinous rock morphed

a cherry blossom
crushed between two pages trace
the wet stain form swirls
characters bring violets
crushed on my vitreous skin

that locust shell
so brittle I could crush it
with one squeeze its legs
and claws falling to the ground
ah if I could slough my skin

these fibrous crystals
their two fold axes mono-
clinic prismatic
a 3.3 density
slough to be diaphanous

to be a spider
eight legs fanned out hanging still
until a flutter
makes me dance round the web makes
me sing the tale of your hunt

Somersault Precedes Transformation

Chorihani, witch-bird, what do you tend?
You bend air and bounce light, a black winged
speck like holes in acoustic ceiling tile.
Come down, you reeling wren. No somersaults,
or I will send every ounce of your
feathered head into that pot by the shed.
You must lend me song until this leg mends.
Where are my cigarettes…what's this? You say
you found a crutch left on the steps of Saint

Nicholas? Go fetch your friends, little wren,
fetch my crutch. I will pay you, pay the way
Manet painted *la Carmencita, mi*
abuela of many greats, cigarette
girl from Spain. You can not see her broken
leg in the frame, only the horse who threw
her when the train screamed by. She warned, *Beware*
the winter wren, for you among us all
retained your shape when the fluff of our wings

crusted and thickened to glue, when the grass
thinned and the wheat dried, when the worms crawled deep
and we shaved the grain from the blade, gathered
it in heaps, these arms nothing but stilted
wings. But you, light, weighed down by no grain, stayed.
I know your secret. Do your spin through this
smoke, bid me watch your jewels your floating skirts,
let me hear the castanets, silver clink
on gold, thud on thigh on ankle. Let me

watch you swirl, your body curl—charm-covered
bangle clanks bead to rib to bead, silk swish
over calf, over neck, the wrist flick whips
jasmine as you beckon and roll, your hair
wound high, locks curled tight, the spin and dip fanned
out, jewels bright lit. Say *talk to my flare, my*
cyclonic pearl—and cresting crash at my
feet. Salome-wren bend my ear to your
lips, say *Grant it* and I will say *Go flip*.

An Ornithologist Ponders the *Zenaida macroura*'s Vanishing Point

Mourning dove, mourning
dove, coo and coo—*Oo-wah-hooo, hoo-hoo*—you
on the top wire
slide to the right, you on the bottom shift
left : diagonal
point, one beak preens, one beak nestles its breast.
Add Venetian blinds—
they still sit apart centered in their own
rows and divided
by an empty lane. Right dove fly left now,
close the distance, but
stay on your upper wire, your blind row
adjacent like cars
one slightly ahead of the other. Both
watch the other birds
flutter back and back, forth from tree to tree
to wire, feathers
and white liquid dropped on car hoods and wind
shields. Both doves face west,
their tail fans shut, sharp tapered lines at right
angles as their balled
bodies morph : first, a sphere; then, a human
heart; last, a child's
toy where a dog-head pops in and out, bulk
dragged along. At times,
bottom watches top, copies bob of head,
grooms the chest spot top
just groomed, but even doves tire of airs :
top dives fast and straight
for macadam, veers to the left, settles
some distance away.
Bottom turns, notes where top has gone, stays, lifts
a wing, pecks feathers,

then stills and watches as the other scares
off a third dove that
tried to land too close. Top and bottom sit,
contemplate the long
horizon and lift off in sudden wing
whir from separate
points, flight paths spread, treasure flaps tethered, wish
bone headed to V.

The Alchemists Dissolve and Coagulate

Two Greek beards profess
fruits turn nuts copier cussed

"Yeah well with breasts they ask
is it the size of a grape
the size of a strawberry
damn paper jam"

to shit to piss if the doctor
asks and what he asks and the proctor says

"It's nice and healthy if it's walnut
sized firm but supple"

and the scholar says

"Yeah if it's walnut size. You know
what they say, You don't
use it you lose it."

Laugh. Clear the jam. Start again.
How funny what gold
to think tumors fruits
the a spot nuts.

sulfur, mercury, salt, fire
air, water and earth, Sol

Luna, copper, iron
tin, quicksilver and lead
antimony, arsenic, bismuth
boron, magnesium

phosphorus, platinum, potassium
stone, zinc, sal ammoniac

aqua fortis and aqua regia
spirit of wine, amalgama

cinnabar and vitriol

decompose : oxidize, digest,
ferment; modify : congeal,
fixate, cerate; separate :

distill, sublimate, filtrate;
unify : solute,
multiply, project
subtle face

At the Academy of Taxidermy Mirram Keeps A Secret

For instance parakeets—
sir please don't touch the ostrich—ma'am please pick up the Sucrets sorry Luden's wrapper you dropped—oh screw it—don't you scoff at me like my dick of an ex-husband Syd—he thinks a woman's greatest sin is one to leave her husband and two to not have kids—only kids I see are the stuffed kind like that room full of joeys—woah look at that boy run to his mum—must have been a Joey—just a taxidermy joke folks—see that Butterga over on that cheap-ass fiberglass branch—my first dance with transformation done in Taxidermy 101—they wondered about those dun-colored eyes but it was B.G.—before glass—and all I had was rice—gee I know what I'll show ya—we keep her in the back—she fights the "play nice" rites—could be because of her past—my dunce Syd claims she had it planned for months—knew exactly when her husband'd be gone but I don't blame her—those men think they have us women fooled—out in a Honda fondling a blonde and they cruise home dinner insistent—he refused to let her eat the tukkeri she cooked so she ran—flew like a loose canary but it didn't bring her peace—always on the lookout for that beast and when the clown found her he hid in a 7-11 aisle while she bought a bag of gummy worms—oh I see your smiles I see you pat your tummies—yes the story splits—people on both sides of Churinga Street say she hid behind a tree stump—the South side say she hugged the stump but they confuse that time on Coolabah Street when the dudes clear-cut and refused to plant new ones—but those who swear by it say she yelled JUMP and the stump got up pulled its roots free and hopped from its dirt strip—leapt right down Bora Boulevard—the North side talk about a pogo stick dumped behind the stump and what the South side thought a trunk was just brown knees and skirt at an angle—the stump's no longer there but you should have heard the neighborhood kids yell "Leap, Yhi, leap!"—Mirram was her name but they called her Yhi—she leapt so far and so long she wound up at the zoo—next thing she knew surrounded and bound and found living with the other kangaroos—they warmed admired her technique her green KangaROO sneaks—showed her some leaps—they hatched escape plans—walls too high—and though her husband never found her some still slap a moral on it like my ornery Syd—he could have at least offered to stay home with the kids—so that's Mirram nee Yhi and we keep her secret—when they brought her in I didn't know what to expect under this skin—but I'll show you this—now don't peek—here in her zipper pouch—look quick—
a shiny new pogo stick!

Circe's Letterpress

She turned
them all to lead
men feet and belly nicks
lined up on the composing stick
the i's

and o's
a's and e's each
letter a face her job
case her reverse harem of lost
vowels

type set
and slugged to make
a spell from line tension
quads and ems brasses and coppers
the string

she tied
round her galleys
rivaled Wonder Woman's
lasso the skin she skimmed off ink
fountains

she formed
into her imps
the tympan packed prints tucked
on the drying rack broadsides struck
mid air

Cave Theory

the spelunker at the cave lip checks
        her gear off
her forehead light concentrated pearl
                on each hand
a glove snug tips cut round belted waist
        tools pick-ax
clamps a rope ringlets bound she puffs out
                clouds shivers
as the cave mouth sighs sedimental
        damp and climbs
in down the rough tunnel-chute she comes
                to a cliff
precipice her pearl light diffuse V
        penetrates
a few feet she anchors rope begins
                to repel
down and down and down a slip and down
        a three day
festival faze she wakes haze struggles
                to part dark's
dress folds wrapped around her every
        muscle leg
works against leg works against leg works
                against leg
the last veil toed off skin sloughed shroud shed
        a pulled off
luminescence one hand jerks around
                the waist roll
to gaze at porous walls illumined
        by fallen
pearl light crevice cranny shadow fed
                by prostrate
body ballooning illumined back
        lit she thinks
monotones like Braque's gray and bronze cubes
                notices
violet cream sighs widens eyes her heart
        beats in time

with the living stone *spe-lunk lunk-spe*
spe-lunk throb
with slitted light pictures dance in red
and ocher
fragments wall hiss depicted growl grass
winds speak hoof
beats rain din moon phases sing *rise rise*
touch our eyes
drawn over eyes rise cradled by her
shadow she
traces a circle inside a square
inside a
circle inside a square cave inside
cave inside
cave inside cave she climbs up climbs out
into night
emerges into dim silver light
now to climb
that hole punched askew in the starless
mustached sky

The Astronomer On Misnomers

Was the silence perfect? Look up and see.
What you see, I see. And yet not quite true.
Sound and monstrous shape. Draw point A B C

D E : Wonder Woman's crown, old Cassie
upside down. If we share this point of view
then there is nothing left to say or see.

But say you saw from Alpha Centauri :
add point F for our sun and the crown shoots
left a zig a zag. Shapes change. Start with C :

how easily it becomes V or B-
flat fifty-seven octaves below, the tune
of a black hole. It's all parallax, see?

Names we make to designate so quaint : freeze
or bang, rip or crunch, they're all big all blue
shift or red shift Doppler Effect and C

is a doppelgänger : the one verse breathes
expands and contracts, a bounce, a blink. You
see I see and what does what we look at see?
A we? Come hear that constant middle C.

NOT *BERDACHE* NOT *GYNANDROMORPH* NOT EVEN TWO SPIRIT

Tonight I will wrap
        myself in newspaper
                columns in cellophane
        packets in cigarette
                butts and moonlight   *I will rise with my wolf face*

Look—dawn now shifts his yawn-glow from my brow to yours.

Today I will ride
        backward into that sky
                only then I who am   *not wife not husband not yours*
        and you who are   *not wife not husband not mine*
                can witness a wingspread

Today I will pause
                and trace your   *scars in a lashed pattern*
        face as it appeared when
                in May you scooped
        buckled legs jaws   *frozen hair from a Route 66 ditch*

Today you will gather
        them, yes, gather them
                today and we will see   *not men not women not even*
        how they react at the green   *megaphonic drums and their loudspeaker*
                font of the Pontiac

Come back under, intertwine your thigh and knee with mine.

At night do you think
        of me alone by the oil   *lamp a spiral notebook paycheck*
                laced water sifting the rain-
        bows for an answer?
                A sand blot.

At night I do not think
                of you I have your   *bills and the deed to a tin chariot*
        arms your legs
                as thought for thought.
        Do not worry.

At night think
    only of our trailer's *cinder blocks pocked with moss*
        narrow bed of our
    village, this trailer
        park reservation.

Look—the Venetian blinds slit our bodies into yellow and blue.

When you go to hunt
        hare on the mill's
    empty lots do you
        think of my heart
    beat slow *like snow covering macadam-cracked grasses*

When you cross
    the rust mound's girders
        into town, near
    the discharge valves you will
        see my eye flash ask *this this is from where I once came*

When you kneel
        beneath the pine
    telephone poles pause
        beside the oak porch
    swings, listen for my voice *in wire hum and metal rub*

Come curl your toes over my toes, and I will curl over yours.

At dawn I will think *the turpentine will weep for you like willow bark*
    of an herb and root
        to place on your
    wound, the paint I will wash
        from your sweat

At noon I will ride *under a foliage of wire awning umbrella*
        into the county back
    ward, I will break free
        dirt I will skin and hang
    siding hides from lamp to post

Tonight I will listen *and think of the skin you once wrapped me in*
for you when I face
the bars where I'll empty
my cup over my hair
as I bathe in the gutter

Look—stillness is not enough to keep your beating wings from mine.

Tonight I will wrap
myself in newspaper
columns in cellophane
packets in cigarette
butts and moonlight *I will rise with my beak and tear*

Rowers

Light frames the boat house
scrapes the oar's long line a gold
        slope a gold edge two
men pull as one snug form hull
oar double slice the water.

Narcissus Resists

Am I the favor seeker, or the favor sought?
Why seek at all, when all that I desire
is mine already?

Metamorphosis of Narcissus I

An ovum broken open the rift
more shadow than separation

an etching a split echo of leaf
five bony petals Narcissus

risen out of shell flipped hair coiled
into roots forefinger pushed out

by strand thumbnail cracked fleshy marble
driven apart stone monolith

balanced on fingertips the tapered
rising a pyramid cone hacked

into a hand and egg Narcissus
a crown not quite a flag planted

shaft cracked but a wave of sinew stretched
kicked up by a released gasp.

Contaminant

Tired of beauty, Narcissus demanded
an end to varnished surfaces, rippled
light. No more would he kneel, drink
from pristine pools or walk the shore
at high tide; he would not chance it
for fear of what the water contained.
And so, at such distance, wave crash
faded into a suck of water over broken
bricks, a trickle down flaking pipes.
The desert burned his skin, shriveled
him until his blisters approximated
and burst into the ripples he sought
to escape. Men still came and ate him,
but now a prune, he had his revenge.

Celluloid

Light flickered across a torn screen
in the movie house where his first
film played. The marquee read *Come
Lie in His Camphor and Nitro-Cell-
u-lose Sheets* : much to the rancor
of bellicose censors who sought
an end to lamé and striped chiffon,
a pre-emptive strike against pink
proliferation. Narcissus never saw
the final cut, so one Sunday paid
a dollar to see his body spread-eagle
beneath a swan head, ass reflected
in a gilt mirror. The reel caught, his
torso blackened, plastic retina charred.

Clubbing

At the Rainbow Inn, Narcissus danced
with a silver ball's thousand rhombs,
the synchronized lights. No black walls
here, but wood paneling, 8 x 10's of drag
queens hung next to *noir* family shots,
and a jukebox for the DJ's night off.
Three middle-aged men sipped beer,
two played pool, a sixth watched empty
rows of tables round and square. A quiet
night at the Inn, the air clear, prismatic,
dance floor empty save for a reflection
caught in a mirror. His eye knew beauty,
knew his body but not his body, the face
that lasts as long as one spun lozenge.

Concussion

Hungover, brow cut from a bar brawl,
skin still flushed from blows, Narcissus
crawled home, unsure if it was daybreak
or nightfall. Light spilled out the slit,
but no wisdom sprang from his split
head. His mind arced off like a broken
rainbow, no keystone to lock indigo
or red, color scumbled into charcoal sky.
Was this heaven-light or his own
flesh radiant? He leapt at shadows
cast on Venetian blinds, eyes half-open
beneath bandage, compress. His mind
scintillant horizon, lined mosaic of shift
and give, of numb, flickering patterns.

Metamorphosis of Narcissus II

A chessboard with no pieces stretched
East the dancer on the stark squares

sleek aloft a red trimmed podium
his contrapasto solo show froze

a water pose : he knew no escape no
way the fluid sudden around

his bones toes rooted arms curled hair wind
blown further West Graces dance

headless a circle the masks flicker
over eight faces eight Graces

flutter and color costume exposed
breasts wanting nothing

more than expansion : elliptic ten opened
what two hands obscured.

Crush

was the name of her hit single. Critics
panned her performance, complained
her voice had echo, too much reverb,
too much feedback. She went straight
to number one. When she showed
at *Virgin* to sign copies, a rush of teens
trampled white flower petals scattered
at her bequest on a pink carpet. Squeals
echoed down mall corridors, around
street corners, the same scene at each
stop until a bootlegged demo surfaced
on the web, showed her shadow voice
lip-synched a digitally-altered, vocodered
track of Narcissus singing *come to me.*

Celebrity Skin

It was not long after the first royalty
check when gossip sought to unzip
the uncut rumors (he was Euro after all).
Webpages plastered posters on virtual
plexi-glass, the photo cropped to hide
his face but to bare a sculpted chest
and those V-hips. The Naiad and Dryad
Sisterhood ripped blouses and button-
downs, beat their breasts raw, cropped
hair in solidarity, and held an on-line
caucus to protest the blatant misuse
of porn. Their anthem? *Friends of Narc,*
the prosthetic cock has firmly docked—
let us unsheathe this innocent's foreskin.

Cut

Ovid's editor deleted a scene : swarthy
man asked *What's your name?* said *You*
caught my eye asked *Where you from?* asked
Do they grow them all so fine there? to which
Narcissus replied *I'm a rare flower* and left
to attend a ribbon-cutting ceremony
in honor of the Narcissus Institute of Skin
and Water, which developed safe razor
blades and bottled *Aqua Dermis*
for athletes and hunters. His advertising
department tried mock ups of Narcissus-
turned-liquid, of Narcissus-shaving-
a-mirror, and *for the first time he traced*
the lineaments of his own face opposite him.

Cybersex

Team Narcissus bought a domain named
www.resistthis.com. Web chat, web cams
in homage to his nightly one-man show.
With no director to yell cut, a web village
jerked and stroked to a lone Narc who
watched himself watch himself on his own
computer screen. He scorned the Golden
Aphrodite Web Ring's gifts to become
the *Venus Narcissus* of the on-line sex
world. A new, strange thirst entered
the pointed corners of his eyes and they
saw this, compared him to Bacchus
and Apollo, strip show gods of yesterday
now dissolved in offline loading light.

Metamorphosis of Narcissus III

A trinity : foreground shore hand mid
        ground water hand back hand hidden

behind receding crags another
        peak peers out invisible lines

connect finger tips at the point each
        ebbs the triangle a fade out

third hand less than second hand less than
        first hand less precise stone harder

smoother heavy with distance cliff side
        weathers away birth groan the light

agleam immediate on thorax :
        black ants scale the wrist one shadow

inch bodies measure apartness what
        touches does not touch earth.

Cruising

Narcissus cruised a dubious fellow
one night who kept light-rimmed
shards of mirror in his sac. He left
our hero to mend the shattered image,
a fractured climax : flesh gave way,
the edge scraped skin, glass cleaved
bone. Hot blood streaked the angle,
white curves; his ice melted into pink
slush, his head, armpits, and groin
wet, raw from a splinter of honey
curls. Before he went blind, his blue
eyes turned purple. His lips locked
his lips, two slivers, jaw-line jagged
edge wed to a jagged edge of light.

Cover Story

Water cut a deal with the tabloids :
catch those cheekbones, parted lips,
the ice blue star in each eye, a simple
first assignment. Narcissus never
showed, so Water froze a faux snap-
shot, afraid of editorial wrath. That
shadow, trapped, proved good enough
to lead; they cut and pasted a crisp
head shot, so early in his career not
a hint of stubble showed. Page Six's
digital grafts gave him some god's
body, edges airbrushed, blurred white
on gray, more light than matter. Any
shadow could shatter that surface.

Concomitant

Neither Liriope nor Cephisus knew
their son was a narcotic; *the offspring*
of rape, some joked, *no worse than syphilis,*
others spat. The glassy, dilated eyes
he caused in all backfired when Attorney
General Aminias' war on drugs kicked
in. Narkissos sent a signed crotch shot :
You are ardent, you adore me, so have
it your way but when the prez's polls
plunged, Aminias resigned, cursed.
Narc's hollow eye sockets stared down
from his pin-up, a double body, a bow
in one hand, a comic strip in the other,
the sun a fanned wheel of refracted eyes.

Metamorphosis of Narcissus IV

The lie of the isosceles triangle
        bisects a receding road curved

ruts double the vanishing point
        as they cut past a villa's terraced

wall : spurned suitor's who cursed Narcissus
        or a foothill town beginning storm

clouds gather here a wedge in blue sky
        frames a parallelogram formed

by fore-finger thumb and egg pallid flesh
        the ghost dog bent in the shadow

a bloody honeycomb in its maw skeletal
        frame : tail haunch and leg bones

muzzle and skin patches caught between fade
        out and material that flickering.

Corporeal

A scar map superimposed on veins led
to serrated treasures, up carpals, tarsals;
over bicep, thigh; through lung, heart
to that broken aorta where a voice lisped.
My scars are beautiful, deep pink. Listen
to their echo—which sounded like the red
blotch of a slap, the thick calm of palms
clutching. Narcisso knew his suitors'
ire, knew his nemesis was not a clone
or evil twin, but that gap in a two way
mirror. *Look on, look through you lab rat*
docs. What op could reconstruct my scars?
Soiled petals grafted, their edge of light
found once more to be action at a distance.

On Clarity

Our young activist released the tell-all
I Am the Narcissus Virus which dug up
Tiresias's sex change med files. Email
petitions—*oust the pre-post-pre-op op-ed*
circulated. Ti blogged back—*You ask*
about dark? There is light within shadow—
know this matter is one of light but *both-and*
went unexamined in light of the verdict :
To know the self equals death? It failed
to force the question. Support waned,
Narc dove to his pool bottom's little aqua
tiles. Chemicals burned his eyes as he
looked up at the sparkle of his image
reflected through light shafts—in reverse.

Crepuscule

A white spider legged its way around
the pool edge, lapped once, twice, three
times by Narcissus. Before the fourth,
it wound a web-parachute, sailed off—
He said, *Spider, go build a web to rival*
the rippled light strung across this surface,
thought, *if I turned first into a willow tree*
second into a carp, and then a young girl
raped by a drunken old man and so became
a drunken old man—swam. Lanai spot-
light and half-moon ooze mixed to form
a sfumato that softened Narc into his
avatar : a corona, a margin stretched out
full, dissolved, a hand-blown pistol.

METAMORPHOSIS OF NARCISSUS V

Ominous a black shadow opens red
earth capped by three arcs middle one

longer than two that flank it object
obscures Narcissus's human shadow

free to roam without the body where egg
flower Graces dance on an icy

ellipse bodies reflect the second hand : warm
siennas and tans sink through water

more grounded by its double egg rougher
outline scumbled a corroded

crack more a gash leaking inky black
a violent birthing in the sky longer

wilder hair in thicker plaits reflected likeness
a swarm of fiery light and speck.

THE METAMORPHOSIS TREATISE

I.

One night before sleep's REM cycles I saw a cockroach. It was the reflection of a cockroach, its actions reversed in the bathroom mirror. Its almond-shaped body wandered down my folded white towel. I tried to tolerate its pin-like head, its over-the-shoulder gaze; spun, knocked it to the floor, rolled up a *Foreign Affair* and smashed it with one blow, "Al Qaeda Strikes Back" stained with guts and legs.

To sleep then. To wake transformed. To have troubled dreams and wake from the dream world to find yourself in a new skin, a new reality. But I did not dream of the cockroach that night, did not wake transformed that morning. Not in the way I dream of spiders. Spiders live in both my dreaming and waking worlds; cockroaches appear only by day as if the scavenger cannot dream the way web-weavers dream, as if gatherers could only be conjured by a waking mind, and predators, another.

I was not surprised with its bathroom debut; Kafka was on my mind. Gregor was not a cockroach, I know. Perhaps he was a scuttering mustache, an easty beasty, those thousand legged lines that scurry from the tub drain, segmented armor that hunts roach and spider. To spare the spider, I also spare the roach. But no, Gregor was not that either.

To wake in a different skin, to shift your form will shift your relationship to the world you once knew. We change the forms we take just as much as they change us. To feel monstrous, larger than you should be, the space around you transformed by your transformation, by your form and shape—door knobs, desks, portraits no longer useful, suddenly in the way. To be seen as vermin, an unclean thing though your shape is neither clean nor unclean; to be an insect, to have the armor to suffer the world, the wings of a beetle and all the possibilities therein.

Beetle, yes. The charwoman refers to Gregor as a dung beetle, *Mistkäfer,* though just plain beetle will do. But wings? Imagine having wings but not knowing you have wings, could use them. Imagine embracing your wings. Would the last cord to your humanity sever? Would the wing-hum, the air-buzz lift you out the window? Would the flight from a room no longer yours but still defining you, the boundaries of you, fade, freed, forgotten?

II.

A cockroach wanders around my desk detritus: sliced-open, scrawled-on envelopes full of half lines, phone numbers, directions and codes; the PBK letter opener flat in its box reflecting the monitor light; mouse pad, mouse, mouse cord; credit card and ATM receipts, package slips and post-its. A headphone cord snakes through W-2s and Vanguard booklets, assorted bookmarks and needle tip pens, jewel cases; it coils around sinus pills, migraine pills, sleeping pills, around the paper clips free from their magnetic holder. A pear-shaped stamp paperweights a green ink pad lid. A plastic dish acts as coin collector, hair tie holder, battery charger. Old Christmas cards cover two copies of Kafka's *Metamorphosis*. The cockroach goes vertical, ascends the wall along the orange, cat-shaped *Schwarze Katze* bottle shadow. I knock it down, and like most times I knock a roach down, it disappears. I sit and type this catalog and as I finish, it appears—no entrance, no herald, simply there—on the cover of an orange folder. I stamp it with the pear.

My two translations, two out of how many, many. As Sontag notes about translation, no longer do we have a definitive version, and always there is the appeal of the newest, the latest. Which of my versions seeks to explain, which seeks to adapt, and do either dare try to improve? How to trust either when, as Bishop noted, "Translating poetry is like trying to put your feet into gloves"?

My Neogroschel translation takes the infamous first line "*Als Gregor Samsa eines Morgens aus unruhigen Träumen erwachte, fand er sich in seinem Bett zu einem ungeheuren Ungeziefer verwandelt*" and translates "*ungeheuren Ungeziefer*" into "monstrous vermin" noting "*Ungeziefer*" means "vermin" and not "insect." Perhaps his preface is in response to my Pasley edition, which uses "monstrous insect." Neugroschel defends his choice as a literal translation of "*Ungeziefer*," for there is a German word for insect, "which is either *Insekt* or *Kerbtier* in German."

And yet, to muddy the waters more, in his famous lecture on *Die Verwandlung* or *The Metamorphosis*, Nabokov argues it should be "insect" since "vermin" is cumbersome and Kafka used the word "*Insekt*" in correspondence about his story. But do we admit supplemental material, the author's comments about his work to explain his work? Divorce the author from his creation. If he intended "*Insekt*" he would have used "*Insekt*" and not "*Ungeziefer*." "*Ungeziefer*" was chosen for a reason, and it has everything to do with the rhythm of the word, of the amassing of rhythm—"*ungeheuren Ungeziefer*"—as we arrive at the end of that first sentence where, in German syntax, the verb resides "*verwandelt*" waking us from the dream to the horror of the dream, when the dream bleeds into the waking world.

III.

Another day, another roach. This one crawls down the bookcase edge. Its proximity to my bed disturbs me, more at the thought of where it will go when I sleep. I know it will not disappear into my dreams. I use the Pasley edition to smote it but as usual cannot find its body. I set a bait trap, resist the urge to clean the long unattended layers of dust, hair, dead skin cells that have accumulated in the corner; I quiet my irrational mind that begs to stay awake half the night moving furniture, mixing a bucket of Murphy's oil soap, scrubbing the floor boards, the wooden shelves, the walls, spraying the baseboards with bottled toxic chemicals that will make me wake with a headache. Stirred dust and fumes.

I wonder after it. Perhaps the stray cockroach wandered off through my body's detritus, the blow merely stunning it like an apple in your back. My shed self coating its armor like Gregor's beetle body when his room was turned into storage, unkempt, unclean space, like an attic or a basement. To become unclean, not because you are, but because others treat you as if you are. To have your room, your living space relegated to an emotional statement. Isolated, cut off. The hidden secret in the back of the closet, under the boxes and old clothes. The buried feelings in the basement, past the empty paint cans and pipes. The crazy aunt, first wife, the trunk locked in the attic.

The charwoman. Outsider, employee, of the home space and not of the home space. After Gregor's last transformation I still ponder the meaning of her words, that "everything will be taken care of." Taken care of in what sense? That everything will work out, be better now that Gregor is gone? To not worry about the removal of the remains, the details of aftermath? In some respects her comment speaks to how Gregor's transformation precipitated transformations in his family. His sister cannot live until he dies. His inability to support them forces both parents and his sister to learn how to support themselves, to return to work, to be self-sufficient.

And to return to Sontag, as she traces the etymology of the word "translate", the across or crossing, the geographic shift of space, the meaning it gained to signify death. Like transform, to shift form, to cross the boundaries of one skin into another. Death of one form, life for the other.

IV.

At brunch, colorful studies of three insects hang framed, one on top of the other, against the bar's brick wall, the beetle's bright blue body dead center. I see you beetle in your garish color, I see you more now than I see the cockroach, but I still prefer spiders and their silken webs, prefer to see your desiccated body with the gray shreds of the last thread.

I think of a repeated line in Frank Bidart's *Desire*, from both "Borges and I" and later in "The Second Hour of the Night": "we fill pre-existing forms, and when / we fill them, change them and are changed—" Perhaps Gregor's pre-existing form was that of beetle, he had a beetle mind and woke to find his mind transformed his physical body, what was inside made manifest on the outside. Perhaps I have a spider mind and claim them as a totem. But what if I woke a spider?

Gregor never looked back, looked behind. He accepted his change, thought nothing of it, tried to continue his life as he knew it, getting up, with all the new difficulties of his shape, to go to work. To fill a pre-existing form, to change it and be changed by it. To never look back, for to look behind brings calamity: look behind and lose your love brought back from Hades; look behind and tower, a pillar of salt.

Beetles, spiders. But these roaches. If only in New York I had the profusion of spiders I had in Ann Arbor. So many, so often, almost one in every corner: the black one crawling across the white carpet; the large brown one by my bed; the pale yellow one at the bottom of the shower. Rescue them, give them space to breath, to eat. In rescuing what shape do I fill? In killing, what form?

V.

Troubled dreams. I woke, at last, from troubled dreams. In the dreams I flickered through the transformation taxonomy, of all the shapes I took and take, the shapes I might be.

There are so many things a human might turn into: a spice, a stone, to spice, to stone. Silent shift. Savory weight. A star pinned to night's chart, a star cluster framing some avatar, or a streak trailing light, fallen, in flight.

But to become night itself, not the absence of light, but a hemisphere that burns even when turned from the sun. To be shadow, become shadow—dependent on lamps, flashes, the day. But not day, never turning into day, the mind as still at noon as at midnight. So be the dawn, be the twilight, live at the threshold of both, of and.

There are other taxonomies, other columns in the taxonomy. Much has been made of a raven or a wolf, so often the human turned into a bird or a creature to be feared. A curse. A hex. Inner self brought to true form or simply the ability to shift at will, choose the shape one wants to take as the mind dictates: I am snake, I am hawk, I am fox. No legs, four legs, wings and claws.

But let us not forget the reverse, to reverse. All the shapes man might become. But flip the equation: not just a question of man turning back, but of the shape becoming man, having never known human form. Could an object know our minds so well? Would its desire to walk and think among us pull it from its state? If my state of mind is stone, is beetle and so I wake a stone, wake a beetle, could a stone, could a beetle dream of man and wake with limbs and lusts?

Past animal, past mineral, the whole vegetable affair. All the flowers and trees peopled by the Greeks, the animals peopled by Grimm. A people's fear manifested in verse: what separates the human body-object from all the other objects of the material world? Where do the surfaces permeate, interpenetrate? A difference perceived, but in such awareness, fear—there is little difference at all. And so origin stories for this plant and that, for the shapes in the stars, for an animal's acts.

And modern man's fears? Machines, isolation. Manifested abstractions. Absurdities in an era forging new myths, beholden to the old. And so to wake a beetle, a monstrous vermin. But one fear never escaped. One change a climax of ever-change: the body's journey from speck to dust, the very fact of age. To age, to watch the body change, not from human to some non-human form, not from one sex to the other, not from one color to another, but the very body's own metamorphosis over the course of life. Size, weight, height. Expand, lengthen, thicken. Shrink. Hair growth, hair color. Hair style, hair cut, hair dye. Hair removal, hair loss. Wrinkles, creases, scars. Aberrant cells. We ink the skin with symbols, pierce and morph its shape. Tighten what sags. Lift what has fallen.

But that ultimate transformation, the body returning to the tiniest atom—will the mind exist in the smallest mote? With no body will it no longer feel? With no brain will it no longer wonder, ponder? In death what might live on, this ultimate shift from one's skin?

I wanted to rejoin the dream, the troubled dream, but found the dream had moved on.

Protean Ambitions

Arachnophobia

Last night, Amalie,
I dreamt a ten-thousand-year-old dream. Light
caught the globes of a hundred eyes. I woke
to a shadow on the sheet, thought *spider*
but not a spider, just my cactus caught

in spot lights from the neighbor's back porch. No
shadow followed Uncle Matthew the day
you were born for no light shone, the power
grid a figment. Some people saw stars they
had never seen and felt their first moon wane.

The spider came weeks later, exactly
when, though…well, who knows when or even how
spiders enter, but beside the garbage
can she sat, the size of your palm. "Spider,"
I said, "Why have you come?" In the angle

between carpet and baseboard, she paused, said
Instinct. The leaves *did* have that rustle when
the wind blew, and the crickets' desperate
song *did* lull me to sleep, but it was not
quite apple time, and so I thought she should

go. "Come, the night is still warm," but she dashed
when I tried to catch her in the Power
Puff Girls milk bottle etched in red and blue
and green. "See Mr. Caterpillar there
on the screen? He makes his own home, knows well

enough on which side to stay." She laughed, perched
on a corner of the kitchen rug. *He*
will return new, beautiful. I have laid
my eggs; let me live out these days beneath
your stove, and under the stove she went. One

hour I spent coaxing her out. A hanger.
A stick. A ruler. Nothing worked. Her eyes winked, flash-
light freezing her body. I should have left
her to eat the Eastie Beasties. But now
she's out in the trash.

Nights in the SKCR : Salutation

Hail spider full of trace caught
in a knot of brown hair white
body spotlight's bright envoy.

Actors table-read Paula
Vogel's *Long Christmas Ride Home.*
Puppets, stage directions chill.

Strand to curled tress spider spins
curious geometries
compares strand to filament.

Her soul's just too big for one
person Aimee whispers, stunned.
Paula resembles her aunt.

Applause. Spider climbs hidden
rope swallowed in beam rafter
shadows. As the crowd mills, thins

a black spider scurries o-
ver floorboards between sandals
chairs : vanishes, off door lip.

Substitutions

One Mother's Day I pinched tissue paper
into a bouquet and when the teacher
said give to your mothers or to she who
was most like your mother I hung the basket
from our neighbor's back door. The phone rang. Sent
to retrieve I tied one green pipe cleaner
to the doorknob, fluffed the crumpled pink sheet.

There is a legend in my family
that when my mother was still a baby
my grandfather allowed a traveling
gypsy band to stay on his land. Their laws
state Rromany never steal from a host
but the family jokes she was swapped out,
exchanged like a Faer folk's swaddled changeling.

My mother like a ruby, the wives' tales
her lips spun : step on a crack and you'll break
your mother's back; play with matches and you'll
wet the bed; drop a knife a fight will brew;
if your ears burn someone's talking 'bout you;
eat pork at New Year's as pigs snout forward;
avoid poultry as chickens scratch backward.

Sayings like incantations, artifacts
to bring luck : turkey wishbones dried, broken
over the kitchen sink; bayberry wicks
on Christmas Day which must snuff naturally;
mornings spent scouring the yard's clover
for four leafs, pressed in *Uncle Remus, Swiss*
Family Robinson, Robinson Crusoe.

But magic? Escape? What would Houdini
say? My mother appeared one October
opal day, he disappeared on the eve
of saints. After ten years, when his wife Bess
ended the séances, blew out the flame,
did she wish one last performance, to swap
body, soul? Return in a glass sub trunk.

Restoration

Cousin Judy's trunk never traveled very far :
its hinges, loose, clacked against tin casing

as my father, palms blackened, lowered it
from the attic. I clutched the ashen cross-pieces,

the itchy, unstitched leather of the split handles,
and set to work. Sanded varnish settled

on the tarnished metal, the freed dirt caught
by tack cloth, cloth which could not clean the dust-puttied

reliefs. So I alchemized, shocked the tin. The in-
laid designs surfaced as the black sides changed

to bright silver stems, fronds, and berry-like
blossoms. On the curved lid, two white and blue panels

emerged with larger blossoms, five-pronged leaves, and veins
in each stem and serration. The pattern

tilted on the front and back panels, stretched
and then compacted, the swollen horizontals

like a folded grid aping giraffe hide. I scraped :
walls, lid, floor lined with yellowed paper, red

faded dashes intersecting green dots.
We thought cedar planks would hide the exposed, knotty

pine, and in my father's garage, we rolled out his
work bench. A ten-inch radial arm saw

winked in the light, the corners of its hood
full of wood shavings that stirred when the mounted blade

spun. The bench lacked doors and hinged leafs, wood scraps piled
against one wall. At sixty, my father

still hit a glitch in every project;
this time, the saw would not cut straight. I gophered : shed

to garage to basement, fetched his canvas bag, red
tool box. Saw fixed, he cut each plank in quick

passes; sawdust clouds spewed out the garage
door, past my car; the hum stuck in trees, echoed off

windows and eaves as we locked cedar to cedar,
anchored cedar to pine with a single

nail gun blast. Brads stitched. Air compressor kicked
in. The loud gasps silenced our sparse conversation

as we varied plank breaks to form an organized,
random pattern, the occasional end

edged with a block plane. Twilight fell. I held
a work light. He leveled, aligned, nailed the last planks,

built up one side, then another and when we could
not bend the planks to fit the curved lid, we

squared it, created a space like a false
floor that held not just fragrant air, but our brief words.

Nails refastened the hinges. We added brackets
to displace the weight of the lifted lid,

opened, admired our work : trunk restored
off nothing more than a frame of thin pine and tin.

Samson in Reverse

Age fifteen or so I rode Metro
bus G home from school, silver
poles, blue plastic seats filled
with teens, book bags. Stopover
downtown and we made room
up front for head scarves, black
and Hispanic women, children—
One day a woman with no nose

rode, sunlight stuck on the flat
bandage tape. Gold G headed
for Allentown cleared quickly
as middle class Caucasian kids
competed to jerk the cord first.
A teenager's power flows from
cars, clothes, hair; if too young
to drive the latter loom and so

the day I was mistaken for a girl
(worse, called hermaphrodite)
I got off on Eighth Avenue.
It was the early nineties : three
years prior Madonna dressed
as a man, danced atop precipitous
stairs in a *Metropolis*-inspired set.
She grabbed her crotch as steam

spewed, as muscle boys worked,
fought, sweat—one found her.
His grimy hand left a smudge on
the sheet in which she wrapped
her naked body. Then *The Girlie*
Show toured and Madge, in tribute
to Dietrich's recent death, dragged
in full tuxedo, platinum pixie-do

hidden beneath top hat, *Like*
a Virgin sung in deep German
accent, book-ended with *falling*
in love again, never wanted to…
A haircut, then, must matter, a do
as boy as boy could be. I headed up
Eighth Avenue to Broad Street
where narrow porch roofs linked

row homes—a tiny cylinder stood
out on one post, candy cane
in flux : blue white red white blue
spiraling up : Rachiele's barber
shop. My mother had cut my hair
one too many times since I last
came here, and Rachiele stopped
mid-snip when I entered to say

hello, like he always did, his voice
deep and soft beneath a thick
moustache. He wore pleated pants,
tasseled loafers, and tufts of chest
hair peeked from his button down's
open collar. I took a seat against
the wall, perused the magazine-
laden table—I liked space images :

suns and moons and black holes;
or sketches and maps of ancient
cities. I did not find the African
women's breasts awful, but
grew frustrated at camera angles,
how men covered their inch or two.
When finished, Rachiele called
"Next!" and asked "How do you

want it?" as he tucked a white
cloth in my collar and tied a long
body bib around my thin neck.
I wanted it shorter, wanted
the shape of my head to show,
wanted no one to doubt I was all

boy, as butch as Madonna
as Dietrich. Silver-eyed scissors

peered from his pocket, leapt
at my head, spoke in accents : *snip-*
squeak, squeak-snip, snip-squeak
and snippets fell, slid down bib—
gold joined gray from the last
customer, red of the man before,
my head light at the sight of the
hairy rainbow. Clippers hummed.

"Look down," he instructed. His
hand guided my head down, away
from the mirrors. Shaved tufts
tumbled as he sheared sides, back,
and then I flinched as the metal
bit. He wiped off the blood drop,
plucked out a brush to dust nose
and neck. He unwrapped me,

conjured a hand mirror so I could
see how the white scalp shone out
above the red line's crusty bead,
platelets piling up. Was it my grin,
the satisfied air? An apology? Did
he see the features of my father
and brother emerge, remember
my first time : I pronounced barber

"Barbara" and delighted in a piece
of bazooka bubble gum given
for silence, for sitting still. Years
since he offered that red and blue
wrapper he offered that day when I
paid. I walked home chewing pink
gum, newly exposed scalp cold,
the nick—brief, small—on fire.

Pilot

Emily before you wrote
        "elephant" and I

        "two black swans" fifty
pilot whales dried into five

lines of perfect penmanship
        no consonants vowels

        just punctuation :
comma comma period

who then led the letter a-
        stray the way an a

        can stray stretched severed
to play nuanced stranded games

one day day one at Dennis
        beach day two flats off

        Lieutenant 's Island
where later those same blond flats

would scroll as Emily I
        scroll to an August

        P-town banner pic
where an Emily age 8

"pours water from a rubber
        boot." Whale skin reflects

        fishing boot fishing
boot reflects whale skin both re-

flect thin arms : boot toe rim held
        above fin. Does this

        Emily know twelve
became a multitude : wet

blankets blessings buckets. But
        just as the crowd rose

        from twelve and twelve had
their one fifty had a one

whose pursuit of squid and eels
        led them to shallows

        tidal desertion
the flooded flats. Skeletal

structures trapped under one two
        thousand pounds collapse

        like preeminence.
Emily post-elephant

I post-scribe to say navy
        sonar causes strokes

        in whales Emily's
father wears his boot fifty

whales died die will die their morgue-
        grave a landfill near

        Wellfleet where I came
face to face with his skull said

disoriented Pilot
        sick Pilot, Pilot

        of pilots there is
no bar for me, you to cross.

Nights in the SKCR : Crux

        Portrait of Crowd Smiling
at *The Inconvenience*
        of Being Born. Self-Portrait
                with Curls Slides and Carousel.

                Not Prostitutes but Amy
        Arbus Slunk Down in Taxi
Cab with Telephoto Lens
        Aimed at Spiked Heels Bobby Socks.

        Portrait of Page in Portrait.
Portrait of Page in Landscape.
        Landscape of Page in Portrait.
                Landscape of Page in Landscape.

                Where portrait intersects land-
        scape a + an X forms port-
scape land-trait : Alien Child
        as Desert Steppe Madonna

        as Street Hedwig as Sun Flare
or Sand Dunes as My Own Chest
        Dock as Anonymous John
                Marsh Lighthouse as Flaccid Cock.

                Other-Portrait as Self Self-
        Portrait as Other raise Saint
Matthew of the Shepherds post
        and bar crossbred the Cross crossed.

Cobalt Bar

Five blue by blue tiles
set at the edge where
blue five by five tiles
          five by three
cover the C. T.
Backboard's adhesive
white stretch grooved goop
spread the way weddings
and dreams of weddings
                    end

for mothers whose sons
and daughters choose not
over ought. (So what
          if he is
forty-nine left his
wife and seven kids?
If you separate
self from selfish root
escapes suffix : fix
                    ish

squarely in the grout.)
Blue blue cobalt blue
not midnight mountain
          nor seashore
showers nor blue route
but aluminum
oxides atomic
number two seven
element sign C
                    o.

(If your heaven is
North Carolina
Appalachia
          and mine North
Atlantic coast will
this Michigan bar
do?) Blue glue blue count
each blue self not quite
aligned despite white
                    grout

in perfect gridlines :
square rectangle strip
ceramic and mesh
          shift and slip
(slippage in today's
world an easy click :
word electronic
word transmission not
words but dresses) a
                    dress

pattern aquiver
on our two by four
supported base green
          square head screws.
Board on board blue tiles
cascade alongside
across our bar. (We
know at the day's end
construction is all
                    quip.)

Sitting in a Wawa Parking Lot

I eat a six inch sub and watch the swan
cross the intersection cars north to south
south to north they slow down pause
exhaust puffs trail off east-west stirs
I study the town-house development
across the way and note how oregano
does not overpower the honey-smoked
turkey as sloped roofs their speckled
brown shingles slide down the beige
siding into faux sandstone and white
trim each unit part of a cluster four
peaks and a pause four newly planted
trees four driveways SUV Saab Jeep
agleam streets named Fireside Raven's
Crossing white cement sidewalks clean
weed-free but oregano and pickles add
a break like sweet peppers to turkey's
monotony I made this without speech
each part chosen on a glowing screen
size bread meat fixings a kid Topher
makes it with one word 30 not even
a word the number so much more than
my place in line wanting to be so much
more 738 Days Injury Free hung above
meat counter free since their last injury
or on this hill near sprawl 738 Days
Since We Opened since arrows traffic
sensors and lanes transformed a country
road four corners of plenty intersections
named "meeting-house" "town square"
the strip-malls screening freshly paved
back roads with shiny D.O.T. signs
where sexless deer have anatomy added
enlarged with a black magic marker.

An Hour After the Meteor Shower

Three blue numerals illumine the room.
        You shiver, chilled from the fallow corn field.
We slip through the gloom, this electronic
        twilight torn from NASA's scrapbook of Neptune,
or the light from one of its cold moons
        exposing towel craters and sheet plains.
Who knew matter would look like this, would take
        on light, a sudden streak, would feel like this,
reveal a body nine planets away,
        when all the light we thought that mattered was
three planets aligned. What does the question
        of life matter so far from the sun? Why
not continue to Alpha Centauri
        or another close star, find a planet
to settle, start our lives over, forget
        the dark past, the path it took to get here,
light years away. All we would have is this
        room's pale light as guide, its stained navy sheets,
squeaky bed, boxer briefs, jeans, the turquoise
        towel on the floor, two brown locked on two
blue as they orbit not each other but
        morning's ciphered blur.

Sketch and Pentimento

Put a pen in my hand and I will sketch
out the terms : before words found me my guise
was pigment, colored pencil pastel yes
acrylic and wood block my canvas name
M D H three letters like two eighth notes
stems connected by a beam but that map

tracks a different theme where the staff maps
clef time and key, ledger and measure sketched
by line and space, rests like periods notes
like words and this time signature disguise
seems to stray from where I started. Erase
then and start again. I was a clown. No

one recognized me that Halloween not
even if I had used a semaphore
to telegraph "last kid standing" my name
forgotten, classmates "who's missing?" sketchy
unable to realize through the disguise.
And if that moment of triumph denotes

love of deception it also connotes
my long standing fear of the red ball nose
and rainbow wig, white face and masked eyed guise
when real skin is hidden, hermaphrodite
face. And yet I love a good drag queen sketch
lip synch and banter but does that erase

or lace a boy too shy to state his name?
These facts are gone replaced by odd footnotes
like you will never catch me in Skechers
or skinny jeans; if you ever did yes
I'd disavow blame my evil twin map
the points my doppelgänger did disguise

to be a spy, a master of disguise
to hide the final claim made to my name.
It's all terra incognito unmapped
dream to be a cartographer endnote
letters all rearranged *I might never*
add that wit or just *might threaten wit* etched

on my final guise stone or urn last note
to preserve the nature-erased name. Yes
a map. But as for treasure? Come and sketch.

Nights in the SKCR : Diabetic

Grizzled balding man in white shirt sits
                    hunched (white bench wobbles).

Alan Dugan floats into pebbled
                    courtyard : *da-da da-*
                              da da-da
                              da-da da
          da-da while Dugan's wife chain
smokes and an ambulance arrives. Ten

minutes earlier man in white shirt
          dozed groaned loud in the pause be-
          tween poems. The gathered painters
                    locals writers cast
                    glances at Lannan
          Foundation reps sound guy two
cameramen focused on Dugan.

                    Grizzled man vomits
          on his left leg splattering
floorboards with a hint of (cheese fruit wine).

A paramedic's walkie-talkie
          sputters now beeps above *da-*
                    da da-da as he
          wheels a gurney over deck
                                        boards.
          Unlatched belt buckles
                                        clink.

Shuffle on pebbles as pebbles slip
          start to fall. Crunch and kick.

          Secured belted down they roll
          across parking lot. Moustached
                    paramedic asks
          How you doin? as Dugan
          finishes to (thunderous
                    applause) : *-kay, that's it!*

Codex Gigas

My many doppelgängers :
I raise my sword *For the Honor of*
Grayskull! pinch my earlobe *Synergy!*
Hail my team *I am Phoenix!*
These clues keys secret identities

The me always receding
Hear me : *who gave you permission to*
Rearrange me like Lavoisier's
Experiment that Muriatic
Acid wash that rearranged
The atoms red rose turned white.
End this. Begin this. Say my
Name. Does its presence make me shape me?

What to do with those who want to say
I have a different name?
Tangled alphabet, illuminate.

Platos de Sal

I. Knit

A cloud of dust on the road—'David's home,'
called Rut Arroyo from her porch rocking
chair. She flipped the knitting, her right needle
filled with stitched slip knots. *Tell him his papi*
needs help in the back field. Rut watched David's
red pick-up pull around the barn patted
her apron pocket—

    Hola, Abuela. Any letters?

            David chucked his back-
pack on a bench, slid his tall frame into
one of his father's hand-carved chairs, thumbing
the opal buttons on his jacket cuffs.
Rut looked up and winked casting off. 'Don't tell
your mami,' she whispered. He tore the red
and blue, Air split from Mail like fingerprint
from skin—paper edge a hairline in his
thumb. 'What news does your Juan send? You're bleeding…'

                  ¿Que? Dónde.

David sucked the flat of his thumb then pressed
it against his knee, the thin letter stock
a blotter between his skin and denim.

    He says the desert is not so hot when you are
        not in uniform, rare
    as that is, and unlike any place he has been—
    more sand than in all those dunes at the shore but no
        grass. A total eclipse
    last month made the light queer—the landscape looked Martian—

David broke off, tried to suppress his lips
and cheeks from their sudden lift. 'You miss Juan?'

    Sí. Who wouldn't? Juan's cool.

'Your mami does not think so, or miss him.'

Mami does not like Juan's
papi, *Viejo* Saul—
'*Viejo Sal*' she calls him but Juan's not like Saul—
if he owned that *campiña* he wouldn't sell it
piecemeal to those *gringo*
developers. No—Juan wouldn't sell it at all.

'No? Look out there, David. *La tierra*—
burnt—your papi has thought hard about their
offers.'

Papi would never do it—I'd never forgive
him.

'He may have no choice with you off
to school—you know he'd sell the whole *granja*
if it would make you Senator Rios.'

Politics. I might
as well just join-up.

'Like Juan? You'd follow Juan that far, into
war?' David folded the letter. A red
dot had bled through and he scratched at the faint
spot on his knee.

We're sort of *juntar*, knit—

'You mean knit like close-knit?'

No,
knit together—*alma* to *alma*. Like a quilt,
or two quilts knit to make
one big quilt, but not bigger, just thicker—not knit
on one edge, but all four, our corners sewn up—two
sides hidden, *dos* exposed.

Rut freed a length of yarn from her basket,
eyed her grandson as she cast on. '*Juntar*?'

Sí—all the patches match, inside out, but inside
they form a new pattern as the patches of one
          touch those of the other—
I know no other way to describe it—did you
ever feel that way with *abuelo* or before?

Rut flipped her knitting, the right needle full—
and what was left became right as her sticks
clicked together, the yarn pulled through a loop
just like Mara taught her. Mara taught her
many things that year at the shore—one time
they husked ears, blond corn silks scattered on porch
steps, in hair. Rut liked to peel each layer
one by one, which frustrated Mara who
showed Rut how to part the sheath up top, grab
hold, and strip the ear in one downward thrust,
the sheath splitting in two layered slips. 'No,
not with your *abuelo*, David.'

          You didn't love him?

                    'Oh I
loved him, but we were not *juntar*.' Rut dropped
a stitch, lost count of her loops, tried to gauge
the row. '*Caray!* Would you look at that? Have
to do this whole row over.' *David, your*
papi needs a hand down back—Rut half rose
and turned to the screen door, 'Let the boy sit
for a minute. *La tierra*—it is not
going anywhere,' and she looked over
her shoulder—David's hands rested—empty—
on his knees. He pushed himself up and turned.
Be back by six for dinner his mother
called, but he half-heard her, thinking of sand
and khaki fatigues and brown skin—sun-kissed—
Rut watched his red pick-up turn, shrink and fade,
the rolling horizon not fields but waves.

II. Field

David sped down the road, his truck kicking
up dust and gravel as he scanned the fields
for his father or the signs of migrant
workers he employed this time of year. His
father, an accidental landowner,
felt it a duty to his roots—*Take care*
of your own, he would say. In the distance
three old willows swayed over the dried-up
creek bed, last year's drought still holding the land
dried post-coital lovers. David slipped Juan's
letter from his sleeve, committed black words,
scratched neatly on the page, to memory.

> Sometimes the night looks like shards of green and brown glass
> scattered on the grass—you remember shooting my
> dad's bottles off the back
> fence—man he'd get pissed, having to buy a new case
> each week at the distributor's. Some of the guys
> sneak it here, but not me—
> I seen what it did to my old man and I am
> not going to let that happen to me. Tell me—do
> those fancy cars still get
> stuck in the mud?

David swerved into a rut to avoid
hitting a Lexus.

¿Señor Navarro? You okay?

'Fine, David. I'm fine.
Lay off the gas—this ain't no race course.' Saul
Navarro stepped from his car, his boots spit
polished, and inspected each tire. 'Good
news for you—no damage.' Old Saul circled
back to his door. 'Can't wait til they pave this
road.' David, hand in pocket, kicked gravel.

Juan sent a letter—he might be home next year this

time? If all goes well?

A news program on Saul's car radio
filtered into the air. 'You would know. We
haven't heard from him in months. If Magda
were still alive—well, she'd probably be
dead of worry by now. Juan done gone off
to war. Carmen back in the hospital.'

How is she, Carmen?

'Fine.' *...a third car bomb exploded today*
killing three U.S. soldiers... 'No one seems
to know. The tests don't, the nurses don't, her
doctors don't—what caused the relapse remains
a mystery while the bills pile up—
you'd think they'd only charge you if they found
something. They charge you just to breathe the air
in there.' *...in a press conference today*
the president indicated certain
reserve units will be redeployed while
those on the ground will see tours of duty
extended six months to a year... 'How's school?
You hear from any colleges yet?'

No, not yet. School's fine—we are
reading the *Gilgamesh* and *Iliad* epics.
I should go—my papi's
expecting me down in the field. Tell Carmen I
hope she gets better and I'll be up to visit.

'You
tell your papi to consider Mr.
Rush's offer bout his land.' David climbed
back in his cab, started the engine—Joe
Henry's voice broke over him in mid-verse
...tell the bed not to lay like the open
mouth of a grave not to stare up at me
like a calf down on its knees... and he drove
over a patch of asphalt close to Old
Saul's land.

They still paving the roads?
Think—a tornado rolls through and you'll have piles
of kindling for miles around—three stories—
bam!—three garage ports—I
think I'll miss the dirt and gravel. Asphalt hum? Not
for me. You and me—we're salt—will always like dirt.

The asphalt smell came at David, triggered
the city, that Joe Henry concert Juan
and he drove up for. He fast-forwarded
to "Scar," braked, his baritone voice singing
What does this look like to you a mark so
fine you barely see you have one just like
it too a twisting vine a mark so fine…
His father's blue pick-up came into view.

III. Bar

Rut watched Mark Hal on his riding mower—
'second time this week' she said to no one
peeling apples over the sink, the red
skins linking up, like double helixes.

          Hola, Abuela—where's Mamá?

'David, look at you—all covered with dust—
go wash up—your mami went to town. Where
is your papi?'

                                                  In the barn still—
          apple rhubarb!

                    'Your favorite. Keep your
fingers to yourself. Look at Señor Hal.
He damn near fell off his mower.'

                              What does he run from? What is that—
                    is that a groundhog?

                                                  'City
people move into their fancy country
houses and yet they've never seen a ground-
hog. I do not understand,' her alto
laughter subsided as she pinched the crust.

                                                  You
          remember last year when we went to the shore?

'Of course. You and Juan were like two gods come
from the sea—two bronze heads, four gold shoulders.
I said to your mami, Look—who would have
thought two gods could come ashore from a sand
bar?' David thought about that afternoon
wave-jumping with Juan, diving between each
other's legs—Juan stood up that one time, gripped
David's thighs on his shoulders as the back

of his wet head nestled David's groin. 'Why
do you mention it?'

Oh

no reason—you seemed happy.

Rut put her left hand
in her apron, caressed the smooth contours
of a painted shell, traced its oblong ridge.
The paint had faded to a barley shade,
but its black and red image remained—an
ornate sandal, footless, straps crossing where
the ankle would rest, a thong for the big
toe. 'The shore makes me happy.'

You used to live there,

no? Before *Abuelo*?

'Yes, after
Eli, my first husband died, I lived there.
Oh, but last summer—you were wearing red
trunks and Juan green. I said to your mami,
"Like Christmas in July." Do not worry—
next Christmas Juan will be home and you will
be home from school.' David tried to picture
it but all he could see was the water,
how it escaped down Juan's bicep's inner
line, down the cleft between his pecs, his abs.
He started to stiffen like that day, when
he had to stay in the water until he
thought it safe to come ashore, and even
then he had to pull his clinging red trunks
off his thighs. 'See—look at that smile. You
know he will come.'

You remember that bald guy who boasted about
the dump he took out on the sand bar?

'And that poor dark fella
in the sling—he could not even excuse
himself for a swim.' Rut rested her thumb

on the shell and began to think about
a stick David tossed, broken end over
broken end into dune-grasses, how she
wished it would have hit that mother clucking
on a cell phone as she spread her freckled
arms with sunblock, her kids chasing the gulls
with stones, water at her ankles, her veined
calves goose-pimply. 'Her name was Mara.'

¿Quién?

'The friend I lived with at the shore. We were,
as you put it, two quilts.'

So
you have felt it—*juntar*?
What—what happened to her—

The sea on nights
of the full moon filled Rut's mind, how moon made
a white stripe in all that silver. 'She drowned,
David. She drowned herself.' The shell, so cool
on hot days, burned now under her thumb. 'Plumb
got up one day and walked into the sea.
It was the year your *abuelo* and I
married. She gave me this the day before.'
David gently took the shell from her hand,
traced the sandal, wished he had a gift like
this. 'The night sea still reminds me—*luna*—
her hair—silver, with a white stripe.' David
placed the shell in her creased palm, a shadow
passing over his face—his papi waved
through the porch window, turned, sat, and took off
his boots, began to read the mail.

I'll take you to the shore
whenever you want—when Juan returns—you, me, Juan.

She turned
the shell over in her hand, traced the red
letter M. 'They never found her body.'
David touched the letter J on his hip,

pictured the D under Juan's fatigues—shore
tattoos. After sun and play but before
the moon they would turn their towels a quarter
to the right laid out on half sundials,
the day traced in sand—no one but Rut saw
them fade in the dune shade their skin traded
for platters of salt—the water needled
her feet, a wave roll delayed long enough
to see sun rays touch the white bar—a rush—
toes sucked—undertow—*Mara* in the spray.

Notes & Conversations

The Epigraphs: I. From the "Proem" to Ovid's *Metamorphoses.* II. From Virginia Woolf's 1928 novel *Orlando.* III. From Jeffrey Eugenides' 2003 novel *Middlesex.* IV. From Philip Roth's 1972 novel *The Breast.*

Orange Colored Sky: Lynda Carter sang this classic jazz standard as the final skit in episode 419 of *The Muppet Show* which aired in February 1980.

Mutatis Mutandis

Bufeo Colorado: Inspired by the Brazilian/Amazonian legend.

Uncle Remus Denies the Ethnographer: For Troy Dwyer. Inspired by Joel Chandler Harris' account of the Uncle Remus tale "Why the Negro is Black."

Aunt Eloe Schools the Scarecrow: Inspired by the 2001 PBS documentary *NATURE: Ravens,* and Charles O. Anderson and Troy Dwyer's 2009 dance and theater piece *Caw.*

Skin Game: "Fashion, like the superhero, celebrates metamorphosis, providing unlimited opportunities to remake and reshape the flesh and the self," from "Superheroes: Fashion and Fantasy" costume exhibit at the Metropolitan Museum of Art, May 7-September 1, 2008. Moments in this poem inspired by Ellen Lupton's *Skin: Surface, Substance and Design.* New York: Princeton Architectural Press, 2002.

Done Gone and Riled Kingston Up Again: The Caribbean bluefish wrasse is a protogynous species where the fish are all born female and the largest and oldest of them are capable of transforming into males. In Biology this is known as sequential hermaphroditism.

Tahitian Women (On the Beach) 1891: See Paul Gauguin's 1891 oil on canvas *Women of Tahiti (On the Beach)* and his journals from the South Seas, *Noa Noa.*

Jade Song Evades the Geologist: Inspired by Cao Xueqin's 18th century novel *The Story of the Stone (Dream of the Red Chamber).*

Somersault Precedes Transformation: Inspired by Edouard Manet's 1862 Oil on canvas, *Gypsy with a Cigarette*, Georges Bizet's *Carmen*, and Konrad Bercovici's "Story of the Gypsies."

At the Academy of Taxidermy Mirram Keeps a Secret: Inspired by the aboriginal tale "The Woman Who Changed Into a Kangaroo."

Cave Theory: Inspired by Keiko Yamamoto's 2000 performance piece *Cave Theory* created through the *Our Shoes Are Red* theater laboratory founded by Devon Allen with music composed by Doug Ovens.

The Astronomer On Misnomers: In conversation with Walt Whitman's "When I Heard the Learn'd Astronomer" and Adrienne Rich's "Planetarium."

Not *Berdache* Not *Gynandromorph* Not Even Two-Spirit: Biologists have coined the term gynandromorph to describe animals where one side of the body appears male (usually the right) while the other side of the body appears female (left) demarcated by a sharp line down the center of the body.

Rowers: See Thomas Eakins' 1872 oil on canvas *The Pair-Oared Shell.*

Narcissus Resists

"Narcissus Resists" is a hybrid text: one long poem divided into fourteen sections spliced with five meditations on Salvador Dali's 1937 oil painting *Metamorphosis of Narcissus*. The fourteen section form is inspired by the "corona" or "sonnet of sonnets" as portrayed in Christina Rossetti's "Monna Innominata" and Lady Mary Wroth's "A crowne of Sonetts dedicated to Love." Ovid's original tale of Echo and Narcissus may be found in Book III of the *Metamorphoses*, two translations of which proved invaluable to the genesis and composition of this poem: the 2004 Charles Martin translation from which the epigraph comes; and Ted Hughes' 1997 translation found in his *Tales from Ovid*. The ghost of T. S. Eliot's "The Death of Saint Narcissus" also haunts sections of this poem.

Celluloid: See James Bidgood's 1971 film *Pink Narcissus*.

Cut: Italicized language taken from Jeanette Winterson's 1989 novel *Sexing the Cherry*: "I began to walk with my hands stretched out in front of me, as do those troubled in sleep, and in this way, for the first time, I traced the lineaments of my own face opposite me."

Cybersex: To return to a source, Angela Carter writes in her 1977 novel *The Passion of New Eve*: "So, together, we entered the same reverie, the self-created, self-perpetuating, solipsistic world of the woman watching herself being watched in a mirror that seemed to have split apart under the strain of supporting her world."

Concomitant: See the pencil on paper and paste-up work *Narkissos* by Jess, started in 1976 and finished in 1991, and found in the SFMOMA.

Corporeal: Language incorporated from Maurice Merleau-Ponty's 1964 essay "Eye and Mind" from *The Primacy of Perception*: "Light is found once more to be action at a distance."

THE METAMORPHOSIS TREATISE

See Franz Kafka's *Die Verwandlung*. The translations mentioned: Joachim Neugroschel's *The Metamorphosis, In the Penal Colony, and Other Stories*, New York: Scribner, 1993; and Malcolm Pasley's *The Metamorphosis and Other Stories*, New York: Penguin Books, 1992. See also Susan Sontag's 1995 essay "On Being Translated" from *Where the Stress Falls*, New York: Picador, 2001 and note 106 on page 314 of Elizabeth Bishop's *Edgar Allan Poe and the Jukebox: Uncollected Poems, Drafts, and Fragments*, New York: FSG, 2006.

PROTEAN AMBITIONS

ARACHNOPHOBIA: For my niece, Amalie Rebecca Hittinger.

NIGHTS IN THE SKCR : SALUTATION: For Aimee Pelletier.

SUBSTITUTIONS: For my mother, Joyce A. Hittinger. Houdini had a famous illusion called *Metamorphosis* which used a substitution trunk, or sub trunk.

RESTORATION: For my father, Raymond C. Hittinger, and our cousin Judy Pettit, for the trunk.

SAMSON IN REVERSE: A transformation in conversation with Elizabeth Bishop's "In the Waiting Room," and Muriel Rukeyser's "Boy With His Hair Cut Short."

PILOT: For Emily Rosko.

COBALT BAR: For Megan Newell.

AN HOUR AFTER THE METEOR SHOWER: For Brian DeMarco.

CODEX GIGAS: Snippet of lyric from Erykah Badu's song "Certainly" off her 1997 album *Baduizm*.

PLATOS DE SAL

Inspired by the *Book of Ruth*, in particular 1.14-22, 4.7-8, 4.15; *Samuel I*, in particular 14.1-46, 18.1-4, 19.1-7, 20.1-42 and *Samuel II*, 1.19-27. Also inspired by a line from Anne Carson's *The Beauty of the Husband*: "as the soul of Jonathan was knit with the soul of David" in section XVI. Detail as a Reticent Event. Joe Henry lyrics from the songs "Stop" and "Scar" on his 2001 album *Scar*.

Acknowledgments

Thank you to the editors of the following publications for giving these poems a first go in the world:

Assaracus “Skin Game”
Clementine “Not *Berdache* Not *Gynandromorph* Not Even Two Spirit”
Barn Owl Review “Jade Song Evades the Geologist”
Blue Fifth Review “Circe’s Letterpress”
The Concher “Cobalt Bar”
DIAGRAM “Samson in Reverse”
DMQ Review “An Hour After the Meteor Shower”
Ganymede “Orange Colored Sky”
Memorious “Cave Theory”
“The Fresco Worker Appears Suddenly in the Picture”
OCHO “Bufeo Colorado”
“Done Gone and Riled Kingston Up Again”
“Bamboo Tattoo”
“The Astronomer on Misnomers”
“Arachnophobia”
“At the Academy of Taxidermy Mirram Keeps a Secret”
“Restoration”
Poets & Artists (O&S) “Somersault Precedes Transformation”
“Sketch and Pentimento”
Ouroboros Review “Aunt Eloe Schools the Scarecrow”
“Substitutions”
qarrtsiluni “Local Lepidoptera Adopt Municipal Pool for Epic Opera Debut”
“Uncle Remus Denies the Ethnographer”
Scythe “Sitting in a WaWa Parking Lot”
The Smoking Poet “Rowers”

An earlier version of this manuscript was a top five finalist for the 2008 New Issues Poetry Prize as judged and selected by Carl Phillips, and a finalist for the 2009 Marsh Hawk Press Poetry Prize.

“Somersault Precedes Transformation” and “At the Academy of Taxidermy Mirram Keeps a Secret” were each nominated for a Pushcart Prize.

“The Fresco Worker Appears Suddenly in the Picture” was included in the anthology *Best New Poets 2005,* edited by George Garrett and Jeb Livingood. Samovar Press, November 2005.

“Orange Colored Sky” was included in the anthology *Ganymede Poets, One*, edited by the late John Stahle, 2009. “Orange Colored Sky” was also turned into a limited edition broadside, designed and printed by Taelor Reid at the Center for Book Arts in New York City to commemorate the June 3rd 2009 reading of the Center Broadsides Readings Series.

“Aunt Eloe Schools the Scarecrow” was included in the anthology *A Face to Meet the Faces: An Anthology of Contemporary Persona Poetry*, edited by Stacey Lynn Brown and Oliver de la Paz. University of Akron Press, February 2012.

“The Astronomer on Misnomers” was included in the anthology *Villanelles*, edited by Annie Finch and Marie-Elizabeth Mali. Everyman’s Library, Pocket Poets Series, March 2012.

“Codex Gigas” and “Crush” appeared on Jeffery Berg’s blog *jdbrecords* in honor of National Poetry Month 2010 and 2011 respectively.

“Orange Colored Sky” and “Samson in Reverse” were performed by actor Sam Breslin Wright in the March 2011 “Lions and Lambs” edition of the *Emotive Fruition* reading series, curated and directed by Thomas Dooley.

“Skin Game” and “The Alchemists Dissolve and Coagulate” both appeared as examples for my prompt “The Poetics of the Mash-Up” featured in the “Celebrity Poet” corner at *Read Write Poem* (October 2009).

Composer Randall West set the texts of “Skin Game” and “Not *Berdache* Not *Gynandromorph* Not Even Two Spirit” to music for the Chicago-based vocal ensemble VOX3. The art songs debuted in January 2011.

Composer John Glover set the text of “The Astronomer on Misnomers” to music. Performed with flutist Andrew Rehrig for the NYsoundCircuit in April 2011.

“Narcissus Resists” was published in chapbook format (February 2009) by Didi Menendez under her Goss183 imprint at *MiPOesias.* It exists in an online format with audio at *www.resisthis.com* and features cover art by Constance Brady. It was a semi-finalist in the 2005 Frank O’Hara Award Chapbook Competition, was an “Also Notable” top five selection for “prowess in composition and daring originality” in the 2006 Caketrain Chapbook Competition, and had won the 2007 Beauty/Truth Press Chapbook Competition.

"Platos de Sal" was published in chapbook format (March 2009) by Ron Mohring at Seven Kitchens Press as the second title in his Editor's Series and features cover art by Lori Hayes. It was a runner-up in the 2007 Frank O'Hara Award Chapbook Competition, a Finalist for the 2007 Keystone Chapbook Prize, and a Finalist for the 2008 Robin Becker Chapbook Prize.

Deep thanks to Sibling Rivalry Press for taking such good care of their authors, for taking a chance on this project, and for all their hard work helping deliver it to the world. Bryan, Chris, Philip: John Stahle would be proud.

For your iconic work: Michael DiMotta and Maeghan Donohue—master image-makers in sister genres.

For your humbling words of endorsement, my blurbistas: Mary Biddinger, Troy Dwyer, and Cynthia Hogue.

For providing the opportunity to give some of these poems and sequences a public life and audience: Sharon Dolin, Thomas Dooley, John Glover, Didi Menendez, Joe Milford, Ron Mohring, Randall West.

For their support, friendship, collaboration and laughter, wine, food, eyes and ears over the years: Cory Clark, Eileen Conner, John Cox, Brian DeMarco, Maeghan Donohue, Troy Dwyer, Lori Hayes, Justin Holden, Brian Lillard, Rachel Losh, Ray McDaniel, Kei Miller, Rachel Nelson, Megan Newell, Emily Rosko, and Emily Wong.

For keeping me sane and grounded, and for being my "first eyes": the one and only wifey, Aimee Pelletier; and my orange heart, Michael Ernest Sweet (==). Also special thanks to my supportive parents and siblings, and to my niece and nephew who know Uncle Matthew is just a kid in grown-up skin.

And finally a special thank you to spiders, to Narcissus in all his many guises, to Rut and David, Remus and Eloe, Circe and Wonder Woman, to Madonna, and to my many many doppelgängers...

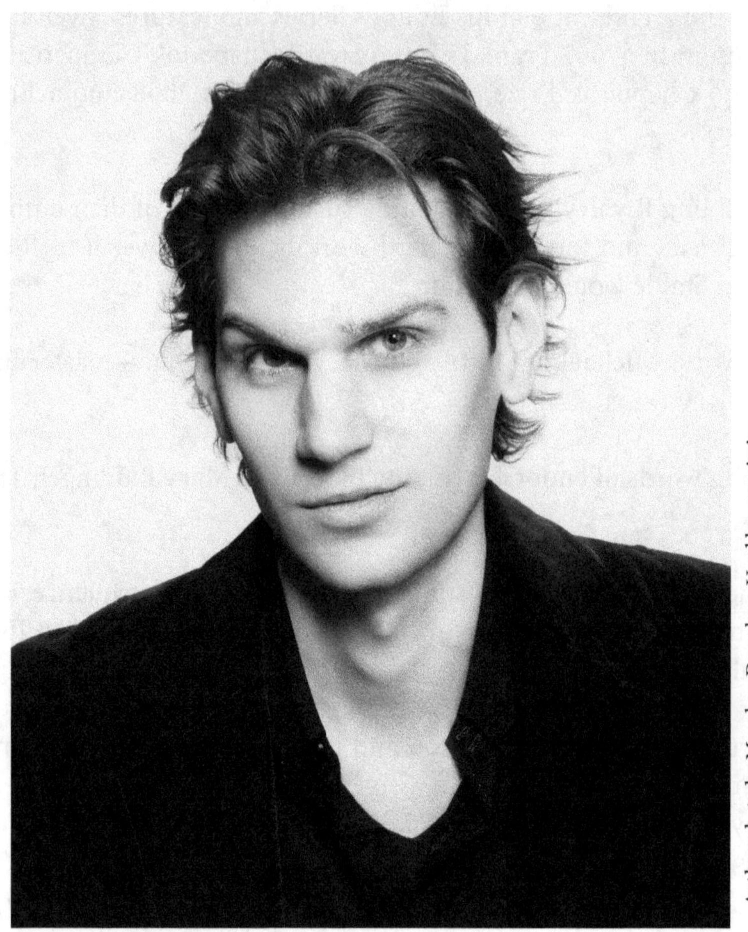

Author photo by Maeghan Donohue. Used by permission.

About the Poet

Matthew Hittinger is an American poet and writer. In addition to *Skin Shift*, his titles include the chapbooks *Platos de Sal* (Seven Kitchens Press, 2009), *Narcissus Resists* (GOSS183/*MiPOesias*, 2009), and *Pear Slip* (Spire Press, 2007), winner of the Spire 2006 Chapbook Award.

Born and raised in Bethlehem, PA (not far from the grave of H.D.), Matthew did his undergraduate work in Art History and English at Muhlenberg College and received his MFA in Creative Writing from the University of Michigan where he won a Hopwood Award for Poetry and The Helen S. and John Wagner Prize. Matthew has received the Kay Deeter Award from the journal *Fine Madness*, two Sundress Best of the Net nominations, and nine Pushcart Prize nominations. His work has appeared in many journals and anthologies, including *Best New Poets 2005*.

Matthew lives and works in New York City.

About the Artist

Michael J. DiMotta is a graduate from Maryland Institute College of Art, where as an Illustration Major, he studied sequential art and illustration. Production design, portraits, architectural renderings, editorial illustration, children's work, and book covers are a few of the many experiences demonstrating Michael's versatility as a free lance illustrator and story-teller. Check out his online portfolio at michaeldimotta.tumblr.com.

About the Press

The mission of Sibling Rivalry Press is to develop, publish, and promote outlaw artistic talent—those projects which inspire people to read, challenge, and ponder the complexities of life in dark rooms, under blankets by cell-phone illumination, in the backseats of cars, and on spring-day park benches next to people reading Alice Fulton and Anne Carson. We welcome manuscripts which push boundaries, sing sweetly, or inspire us to perform karaoke in drag. Not much makes us flinch.

www.ingramcontent.com/pod-product-compliance
Lightning Source LLC
LaVergne TN
LVHW080332110826
845155LV00024B/148

* 9 7 8 1 9 3 7 4 2 0 1 4 7 *